JANE

COMPLEAT

JANE COMPLEAT

poems by

Larry D. Griffin

2016

FIRST EDITION, 2016

Jane Compleat
© 2016 by Larry D. Griffin

ISBN 978-0-9903204-9-4

Except for fair use in reviews and/or scholarly considerations, no part of this book may be reproduced, performed, recorded, or otherwise transmitted without the written consent of the author and the permission of the publisher.

Cover Art
Jane in the Aftermath, 2013. Acrylic on canvas by Larry D. Griffin.
Private Collection of
Hassan Hamdan Al Akim, Ras Al Khaimah, United Arab Emirates.

Cover art and author photo by Eoin Brown

This publisher is a proud member of

COUNCIL OF LITERARY MAGAZINES & PRESSES
w w w . c l m p . o r g

Book Design by Mongrel Empire Press

Acknowledgements

All of the poems in "The Jane Poems" section were previously published in *The Jane Poems* (Winston, Oregon: Nine Muses Books, 2002).

All of the poems in the "More Jane Poems" section were previously published in *More Jane Poems* (New Orleans: Umpteen Press, 2003).

Versions of Jane poems were also included in the chapbooks *Airspace* (Slough Press, 1989) *Greatest Hits 1968-2000* (Pudding House Publications, 2000).

Poems in the "Loving and Longing for Jane" section were previously published in the following journals.

"Arbitrary Alabama." *My Favorite Bullet* 2.2.(August,2001): 17-18.

"Artifacts 2," and "Last Love." *Uno: A Poetry Anthology*. Ed. Verian Thomas. X:IBRIS.COM (2002). 232-236.

"Cigarettes."*Emo: 8* (December, 2001):7-8.

"An E-mail." [Dyersburg, Tennessee}*The State Gazette* (2 November 2003) A-12.

"Late Fall before the Beginning of Winter." *Trepan 3* (Spring/Summer, 2001); 20-23.

"Voice." Lkd. *This Hard Wind*. 5 November 2003.

for Jane

Contents

The History of Jane — i

Jane

Aubade San Antonio — 1
On the Brevity of Afternoons — 2
The Carpet's Betrayal — 3
Eating Jane — 4
Few Women on Earth — 5
Giving After Christmas — 6
This Heart — 7
The Hideout — 8
Home Free — 9
The House in a Place Near the River — 10
I Do Not Tell Jane — 11
Jane Admires the Furniture — 12
Jane at the Meeting — 13
Jane at the Piano — 14
Jane Before her Front Door — 15
Jane beside Herself — 16
Jane Dives into the Swimming Pool — 17
Jane Dreams of Rocks — 18
Jane Dresses Antique — 19
Jane in Alaska — 20
Jane in a Vision — 21
Jane in Austin — 22
Jane in the Exchange — 23
Jane in Midland — 24
To Jane in Old Age — 25
Jane in the Living Room — 26
Jane in the Shower — 27
Jane Steps Forth — 28
Jane Stretches — 29

Jane Swims Away	30
Jane Unfolds	31
That Night in Jane's Arms	32
Jane's High Bed	33
Lipreading	34
Photographing Jane Looking in the Mirror	35
The Poet as Himself and Jane as Muse	36
The Rains of September	37
Separation	38
She Does	39
Sixteen Questions	40
So Much I Looked	41
Tears	42
Telling Jane Why I Write	43
Tryst	44
The Well-Known House	45
Autochthonous Jane	46

More Jane

Fast Past	48
Jane in Bronze	49
Jane Juggles	50
Jane Lives Anne's Life Vicariously	51
Jane on the Frontier	53
Jane Plays "The Nearness of You"	54
Jane Reconciles Herself	55
Jane Refuses My Invitation to Belize	56
Jane Sees the Difference	57
Jane Speaks of Mexico	58
Jane Writes Her Dream	59
Jane's Alarm	62
Jane's First Note	63
Jane's Fortune	64
Jane's Island	65

Jane's Spigot	67
Jan(I)e	68
Memphis	69
More than a Couple of Lines	70
Neither	71
Once in a Blue Nude	72
The Only Response	73
Packed	74
The Passing of Trains	75
Using Frank's First Lines in Attempt to Seduce Jane	76
Val Verde and Beyond	81
When Jane is Jan(I)e	82
Yes	83

Loving and Longing for Jane

Late Fall before the Beginning of Winter	87
Duplicities	91
Further Variations on My History	94
Grandmother	95
Love's Last Lesson: Loss	98
Last Love	100
Cigarettes	106
Jane's Laughter	108
Those Seashells, for Example	111
What the Living Feel	113
Voice	114
Artifacts	116

    1. Prelude
    2. Sports on Television
    3. Madrid Madness
    4. Conversational Exceptions
    5. Refusal of the Proposal
    6. Arbitrary Alabama
    7. Up and Down: The Yo-Yo of (E)Motion
    8. Orality and Orgasm
    9. Traffic

10. Secrets: Confessions
11. An Email
12. Nonfiction
The Extra Poem   139

The History of Jane

Confronting Jane for more than thirty-five years now, I know she leaves me only with this book. Since the beginning with all my limited poetic prowess, I do everything, all these poems, to love her and also to rid myself of her. She remains both a negative and positive force in my life as a poet.

As far as the erotic suspicions of readers who may perhaps enjoy these poems, or not, who discover in either their readings or misreadings, too, please know that I remain indebted to my beloved sister poet Margareta Waterman and my brother poet Dennis Tyler, who agree for the republication of *The Jane Poems* and *More Jane Poems* respectively herein, which they first in their kind wisdom published years ago. It now remains *Jane Compleat*, which my sister-poet Jeanetta Mish feels needs a place in our world.

To other small magazine publishers who have published poems from *Living and Longing for Jane,* the third part and conclusion of *Jane Compleat*, I remain truly grateful.

I apologize for nothing herein, for I never write anything my mother does not read, and my mother read all these poems. She may have been somewhat a less open minded reader than my beloved son, Blake Edward Griffin-Hearn, who also critically read all these poems, but like his grandmother, he understood what this poet confronts. I truly thank my beloved mother and my dear late son Blake Edward Griffin Hearn (1979-2013), who so loved his grandmother, my mother (1917-2007) for their contributions to the Jane poems.

—Larry D. Griffin
Ras Al Khaimah, United Arab Emirates

Jane

Aubade San Antonio

Would she have sex? Please and thank you.
The wad of a wound bed sheet.
One silver earring left on the dresser.

Four possibilities, Jane laughed,
but only two remain vertical. Now, I said,
silent standing figures shadow the horizon;

movement manifests its (e)motion in memory;
and, we'll both feel that toe tingling curl
of moist music and lavish mausoleum.

You did whisper, Jane whispered, tongue in ear,
that will wants no warning. Try to make
others make you. Crushed citrus in the air.

You breathe in and out of me
cooling ashes
after a friendly fire.

On the Brevity of Afternoons

When I think, dear Jane, what in all both we've
done in meeting like this in the afternoon
when sense alone could not keep us apart,
then I must allow my soul to believe,
like butterflies escaping the cocoon,
we in our departures create our art.

O now if my fingers could only touch
the tension of your cheek in that our room
(Knowing the other, having been apart),
I could never ask again for so much,
sweetheart.

The Carpet's Betrayal

I can still hear her breathing in my ear.
Jane fulfills my sensual delight, and I,
hers. We rise from that firm floor
and dress quickly without words.
She leaves the house first. I follow.

Walking the uneasy streets, I suspect
betrayal of the carpet that we fell onto.

But I take from there more than I left,
the images re-imagined repeatedly,
their continual resurrection years later.

Eating Jane

O valuable, voluble, vibrant, vagina
viewed from below the vantage v
of victorious legs! When I
bury my head and eyes and
tongue plunges back and
forth and in and out
until frothy lipped both
she and I, Jane pulsates
and throbs her legs hard
against my ears until
pounding all is heard
beyond the muffled pleasured
screams and her bitten lip.

Few Women on Earth

The mirror deceives you not, a true reflection,
Few women on earth have your beauty, Jane.
Your eyes sparkle like diamonds,
your lips have the color of coral,
your teeth pearl, as you smile.
You move in graceful dance on
feet that serve my fetish.
Ah, those hands that touch, that silky hair.
But how does beauty serve?

Locked inside the harem of my mind,
who but I can see you?
Only my lust lingers here for you,
and the loins' cravings harden
my cheerful glance until cold
stares fasten you here in words.
No wonder your heart cries out in pain.
Would you were but my muse!

Had you been born of flesh, not the
figment of my mind, you should
show yourself to others, to all,
so men would admire, women envy
your beauty, both agreeing that
few women on earth have your beauty.
When you drive by in your convertible,
the streets of Dyersburg would jam
with people only to see you go by.

Giving After Christmas

After we fuck Jane and I retire naked
to the living room for after-photographs
before her Christmas tree.
A friend telephones Jane and
while she laughs and talks
(she's on a portable phone
and we're sitting close on the couch),
I play with myself
to remain erect and hard
(she notices and smiles all the while)
for the photographs we take later
without taking anything from one another.

This Heart

From canvas, oil paint will crumble,
watercolors wander away when wet,
aging photographs do lighten and fade,
old statues, knocked down are thereby broken,
vessels develop hairline cracks and leak,
words on pages return back to the dust,
and this my heart, my Jane, will only rot.

The Hideout

Hiding itself from the city streets,
the room was fine and appointed.
From the window you could see the river
broad and brown. Through glass
came all the sounds of the traffic,

and here on the overused, old desk
I wrote a single love poem: I had words,
the power and acquisition there obtained
that I would now so many years
later give anything to have again.

Home Free

I meet you here in the bedroom
after time of belief in kitchens
and the outside world those days.

You are baked and black. I feel
the knowing of wood stove heat
that night and dreams come forth.

Dreams fade from and to factories,
what I worked when I lived some
few years ago in this mill town
with its chamber of commerce
and its prosperous, marble banks.

I wandered those lovely streets
and found dust beneath my feet,
but now I see how the sunlight
splits the sky yellow and red.

Sun sets. Moon rises. Bright
stars burst from a ripped sky
here on the edge of Tennessee.

Necessity divides not the universe
from this catalyst pride in all
that can happen here and now:
I take the plow, bite the soil, and farm
the land only to sleep with you.

The House in a Place Near the River

I said, I will go to another place, I will cross another river,
another house I will build, a better one than that.

Your every effort condemns you to your fate. You're too late,
and your heart, like your mind, fills up with heavy furniture.
You had your dry years in the desert, and now it only rains.

Wherever you turn your head, whatever you look upon
materializes into metal monuments or mahogany
crates filled with these samples taken from the ruins,
a representative archaeology of what happened there.

I will find farther places, I will cross wider rivers,
for places and their rivers remain the same to me.
Never I to myself, no more than the houses I build.
I walk the same streets, I drink the same drinks
in taverns all the same, and I worship everywhere.

Always I will go to another place.
I have not the faith for it—
There is no ferry for there is no river.
As for me and this house,
we stand selfsame against the world.

I Do Not Tell Jane

I do not tell Jane
I meet Marion
in Amsterdam.

In the restroom
of the Van Gogh,
Marion stands me
on the toilet seat,
unzips my fly,
takes me from my trousers,
plays me down hard
in the power of her pout,
so that significantly
I shake the stall
before I scream
and then release her hair
entwined in my fingers.

As she licks me off
and puts me back,
all seems sunflowers
and starry skies.

When we kiss and part,
I taste myself on her lips.

I do not tell Jane
I meet Marion
in Amsterdam.

Jane Admires the Furniture

Jane admires grandmother's oak dresser
and says, *The pulls should be
brass, not those white ceramics.*
Still slick with the warm perspiration
of her body, I touch my cooling wet breast
above my heart, feel its dampness
with my right palm, let my eyes
dance across her lithe naked body,
recall the joy of the adjacent shared bed,
the floral sheets still in damp twists,
and search the mental hardware stores
for the right handles to match the bed's
brass, detach the old, install the new,
noticing never the push of her words,
and only feeling the pull she has on me.

Jane at the Meeting

After Jane is promoted,
she attends too many meetings:
She protects the groundwater.

She recalls that
one fourth of the nation's
homes use septic tanks.

She's good with figures,
has a good one herself,
but you know how love goes.

When psychic insights lack
physical endeavors take up the slack.
She does not own her rhyme.

Going to the gym an extra day
a week is not enough;
she wants astrology.

She wants her palmist
to explain the lines
in her hands.

When she tires of the talk of buffers,
she remembers the *I'm a lumberjack*
song:

*I sleep all day
and I sleep all night—*
until meeting's end.

Jane at the Piano

A light breeze through the open door:
Jane nude at the piano.
Her round buttocks flat
against the hard bench.

A cursory hearing
of the musical notes:
What was it she played?
What mattered was she did.

Until, wandering to other rooms
I heard her stop, comment
on the keyboard action,

this: the poem I wrote
that shows I heard.

Jane Before her Front Door

Against the tortuous turquoise trim and
the dark mad magenta of your front door,
the sun behind me across the dry creek,
your back to the wedged West,
the shadow of your happiness
you cast against your despair.

Jane beside Herself

Jane is so beside herself
that she finishes off the glass
of white Zinfandel,
her recently-satisfied me,
and the morning paper.

Through the silver screen
of the open storm door,
she hears the mockingbird,
whose sound she translates
first as *praise* or *blame*,
and then as *wild* or *tame*.

Jane Dives into the Swimming Pool

In the plunge Jane
dominates the surface
by breaking wet into
splash, circle, and
concentric, radiating
ripples that erect her
nipples hard away
from the aureoles of
her breasts in the light.

In the push upward, Jane
submits herself to the water.
She controls her abandon.
She abandons her control.
Momentarily in erotic embrace
of water, out of time, without
gravity holding her down,
Eros and Thanatos
oscillate toward equilibrium.

In breaking the surface,
Jane sucks hard to fill
her lungs with air, as
in the ecstatic aftermath
of fucking me. *Elle
meurt a chaque minute*.

Jane pulls her hair back
over her head. She with
perfect strokes crosses
the pool and climbs the
ladder. Water beads
on the beauty of her
buttocks. Just a quick
shake of her ass as she
steps off the ladder. In
this immediacy of this
mortality, I have her *encore*.

Jane Dreams of Rocks

Jane dreams of rocks and water,
how one may dissolve the other,
move them from one place to another,
enter a crevice, freeze, crack,
and split, roll and tumble,
smooth and shape, into spheres,
perfect, like falling drops of water.

Jane Dresses Antique

Jane dresses in her grandmother's dress
and says, Her waist was smaller than
mine. She was much shorter too.

I try to summarize her prologue
by saying, What's past is past.
The future folds out from the present.

Jane laughs, Reality is its own
excuse for being. Help me with
these hooks, would you please?

I'm better, I say, in taking things
off than putting them on. Now
where did I leave that cigarette?

Jane says, I appreciate your
genius for the inappropriate,
but I just can't wear this.

When I ask why not after
telling her how well she fills
the shape of the dress,

she answers, It's tight, too
tight, and in retrospect I'd
much rather you undress me.

Here we go again, I think,
and Jane smiles and says
aloud, Yes, here we go again.

Jane in Alaska

All I know of Jane in Alaska
shows up in the slightly blurring
single color photograph of her
there. She wears light blue
coveralls, her name stitched
JANE in black embroidery
above her, my favorite, left
breast. Her long brown hair
falls from under the silver
aluminum of her hard hat.
Thick gloves hold her tender
hands. Heavy black boots
shoe her tiny feet. She looks
straight into my eyes, or
rather into the camera. Her
famous smile creases
parentheses around her
mouth continuing a motional
muscular behavior that will
wrinkle wonderfully around
her mouth until all she says
is powerfully parenthetical.

Against a background of white,
pure white snow, resting her
weight more on her right leg than
on her left, her right arm
akimbo, Jane loafs there
an erect snow angel,
a cipher in the snow,
a hieroglyph on bleached papyrus.

And as always, I want to be her
Champollion, to translate her over
and over and over again forever.

Jane in a Vision

Certainly this black and white photograph,
billfold size, resembles her.

Quickly taken, on the Capitol lawn
one bright Austin afternoon.
A hero's statue looms behind her.

It resembles her. But I remember her more beautiful.
She was sensual to the point of panting afterwards,
and her hot breath filled the July afternoon.
In my memory she remains more beautiful
now that my heart holds her out of time.

All of that was then. All of this now too old,
the photograph, the lawn, the afternoon.

Jane in Austin

Perils and perfections everywhere.
Praise of the bohemian life.

The singers and the dancers
on Sixth. Coffee shops and boutiques.

All the conversations with Susan.
What George or John thought.

Dancing the two-step at the Broken Spoke.
Alvin Crow on the fiddle.

And where is the result? She remains
uneasy. I have some suspicion.

Her counselors unrenowned for wisdom.
Our history, she thinks, has gone too far,

and its end demands immediacy.
Jane returns once again to read

of how to do it from her book;
there in a loud voice, not quite her own,

she chants almost as if the words were holy:
Perils and perfections everywhere.

Jane in the Exchange

Joy lessens not in the speaking of it.
And delights seldom remain silent in the heart.
They thrive in getting out and into words.

Jane loved me and I loved her.
And she vowed never to love another.
But she is so beautiful and often pursued.
Intending to find pleasure, to learn more about love,
that is why she found herself in another's arms.
She desired to become an artist and a scientist one day
and then return to me with her heart at ease.

A year had not passed before her mother died.
Fires raged in the countryside. Whatever we had
we invested in the derivatives of a failing exchange,
sold off our precious moments like discounted jewels,
until only our song was left. Our failure
became tabloid talk. News spread throughout
the states, and the more righteous, claiming
the name of friend or acquaintance, looked on
her with eyes that betrayed their lust.

I was not writing. I was not painting.
I stayed late at the office every night,
where I manipulated the data to set
it right, but failure compounded failure—
the beating of hammers on unmalleable
metals—until the one who held her,
smarter, richer, more handsome, won her
and held her heart against harm's way.

And her soul grieved in her loss and gain,
and I held my tears as I held my judgement.

Jane in Midland

In the room of the poet, his room
hung with images of conquest, she
finds the warmth of his bed with
light flickering from the diamonds
in the rings on his fingers, and

both wearing nothing, she goes down
to her knees before him, and takes him
in her mouth between the mirror
silver and the black iron bed.

His English is standard and pure,
but a slight accent betrays Oklahoma.
He confesses his love to her there,
but she is too blue to hear and
still grieves the loss of her husband.

She hears his voice, but not his words,
and that soothes her into the softness
of his sheets where they fuck for a week.

To Jane in Old Age

That sweet song I sang, Jane, was an old one,
its title now on the tip of my tongue,
but only the hearing of such old songs leads
again to memories when we were young,

when all our wants were also all our needs,
and all our laughter filled up our throats,
as the righteous wind whispered in the reeds
beside the green lake where we made our deeds,

studied solid studies, and made nude notes,
mine in the coarse, yours in the simple fee
of lovely hips moving on castoff coats,
while you whispered in my ear all those quotes

of how you lay there making all of me
all naked in your choreography.

Jane in the Living Room

Not until she sees the clouds
through the uncurtained window
move across the Tennessee sky

does she find comfort in
the sparseness of the room.

She knows not what happened.
Arousal determines appraisal.

When she hears the squeaking
of the old oak floor, she is neither
unapproachable nor alone.

Jane in the Shower

Water beats and beads on the border of her body,
so that skin, pores open, glistens golden in quiet
clarity of light before steam softens visual sharpness
to sweet subtlety of hands grasping yellow soap she
lathers into white suds that foam her perfect breasts,
bright nipples erect like luscious strawberries,
her hands then smoothing soap between her legs,
so that in the counterclockwise suck and swirl,
she laves away my sweat and semen and is left
only with the inability to ever lose that nostalgia
she has for all my touching her with all of me.

Jane Steps Forth

She stands before the light
so that her shape shows
in pink silhouette
through the fine folds
of the sheer fabric,
a lined linen that
she lets fall free
from her fragile shoulders
into a simple pool
upon the seasoned parquet
from which she slips
her foot loose from the folds
and steps forward
into my senses forever
that soft and sad September.

Jane Stretches

When Jane stretches into the dark
of the well-made bed,
    I take her
hand in my hand and kiss it.

The bats in the chimney return
from their nocturnal feed.

Morning light fills the windows,
so the bedroom warms,
like this, my beating heart.

Jane Swims Away

Jane rocks back and forth in water,
wet with the will to swim forever,
and when she finishes her last
fine stroke, she hears squeaking
in the clouds above her head.
Later after pulling herself pool side,
she towels herself off, looks for her
sunglasses, finds them on the chair,
puts them on, stretches out there
on the chair, and closes her eyes.
Sun soon warms her brown skin.
She dozes, sleeps, and then she
dreams of rocking back and forth
in water, swimming forever under
a sky without the least cloud and
in a pool so large she cannot see
the edge, but she knows she no
longer needs sunglasses, towel,
chair, or me to finish her dream.

Jane Unfolds

With your forearms triangulated
so that your elbows rest before you
on the broad, damp white sheet,
you sit cross-legged on the bed,
leaning forward toward me,
your chin cocked to your right
shoulder that your hair cascades
over, and looking up to me
with those eyes, so that I see slits
of white between irises and lids,
you rest your chin on the fingers
of your right hand that grasps
loosely your left clenched fist.

Wrists block your breasts from sight;
feet you've tucked in to hide your sex;
skin still glistens from the last time.
Definition of your left arm tantalizes,
and your lips start toward a smile
before your command, Fuck me again,
opens them, and you unfold, uncross, and
roll fast into my arms all open once more.

That Night in Jane's Arms

All night long Jane held me in her arms,
so that I was hard in longing against her.
She brushed my cheek with fingernails
and asked, Will this be another of those
I want to fuck you poems or some other

serenade before you tell me of a mountain,
the aspens shimmering in autumn, as if
hung with gold coins, not the golden
leaves catching the light, and why you
brought me there alone this time of year?

Now I bring you here this time of year
alone, for whom else could I get to go,
and what the light shines for you
depends upon where you cast your glance.
I'm not leaving this or anything to chance.

I want to fuck some other or you, and poems
acquire their own seduction in being done.
When I press your nails to my cheek, I speak
of that longing in my heart, your body willing,
all that long night you hold me in your arms.

Jane's High Bed

Jane's pleasure screams
down the wall of her
bedroom from her high
bed. I take my tongue
from between her legs,
lick my lips, tasting
her until I smile, then
swallow, and fall back-
wards hard. Her duck
downy feather pillow
catches my head.

Jane's already over me
down there on her
knees at the foot of her
high bed. She has me
in hand with both hands.
She wets her right middle
finger with the finesse of
her lovely lubricants,
inserts it in me, chuckles,
and fingers me in and out,
matching her made (e)motion,
while with her left hand she
strokes me firmly, quickly,
rhythmically, into the solid
suck of her lips and mouth.

Fiery commas explode
from my vision's edges.
Jane says, There's so
much I can't swallow.

Lipreading

Beside a river in an old city, Jane,
I once drank with you at a small cafe
a good coffee made better by fresh cream.
When your spoon plunked against the china plate,
cathedral bells sounded forth loud and long,
so I could no longer hear what you said,
your red lips moved in a silent movie,
and I swear even now you spoke of me,
what you hoped to achieve before dead
silence then followed forth to prove me wrong
about your story, the season and date
of that little bit of refreshment dream
long ago when you finally had your say,
as you had my heart, but with no pity.

Photographing Jane Looking in the Mirror

As Jane looks at herself
in the silver mirror and
reflects on her nudity,
I peer through the camera's lens,
capture beauty contemplating beauty,
before shutter click (shudder
clicks) and fastens her
t/here Fuji-fast forever.

The Poet as Himself and Jane as Muse

The Poet as Himself

What limitations did I set for myself in choosing
you without recognizing that you chose me?
My words fall on the page like empty husks, and
even the pretty ones betray your complicity.

Should I seek the secure sentiments of the soul,
the reward of virtue being only virtue?
My continual discouragement drives me always
to the joy of your arms and the pleasure of your body.

Alone, the heart, cold in its craft, seeks only
another, yours, so that its songs, my poems,
compromise the clarity that pure avarice,
at least admitted, lends to the length of our lay.

Jane as Muse

Your eyes see the clearer vision. Your heart
remains true. Only the words of your songs
contain the truth, and in your loving me,
what besides your words can contain us?

You divine meticulous moments, recall from
them indelible memories, from which you
take joy, like your pleasures with my body,
and what you make once lasts forever.

If the heart holds out for its own acquisition,
fear not. No more think any less of
yourself than I always think of you.
Reward remains close, because I am near.

The Rains of September

Now in the dampness of this bottom,
awaiting the rains of September,
I list on a small scrap of paper
the realities of tragedy, the un-
said word, the mis-spent dollar,
the day stolen from vacation
years ago, the crash of china
plate to hard wood floor,

and if in this moment I call out
your name, Jane, what I should
have done then, in doing it now,
what health does this show of
the heart as all the cells
of the skin desire water:
The damp warmth of dancing
in the rain before saying good-bye?

Separation

We both were hurt in our parting.
We did not want it; it was late.
The needs of living obligated me then
to this distant state— Tennessee.
Our love now becomes something else;
her attraction for me diminishes, like my dollars;
my attraction for her, great as the miles apart.
But we did not desire this final separation;
it was fate and it was destiny,
those articulate artists, that separates us
before fires cool, before time ages us,
so that each remains forever what they were,
beautiful or handsome, hot for the heat
of one another.

She Does

She does not tell me what to do;
when I dance wrong, she steps on my toes;
when I speak newspeak, she suspects me.

When I inhale, she breathes in.
When I stop, she really begins
to think about what I thought,
and then we know we are friends.

Hanging around the pool, I like all of it.
When Charlie Chaplin joins us there
in his clown dance, his painted mustache

tickles tales from both our lips, trips
us into fantasies we never flopped before:

Gracia a la vida!
The old joy of life,
the standing up,
the falling down—
love in front of
a candy store.

Sixteen Questions

What holds you back?
The back I hold?
What do I lack?
Whom have you told?

Is it in your eye?
Or in your voice?
Could you just die?
How else rejoice?

What of the past?
That too will pass?
What of the last?
Is the clay cast?

What do you see?
What have you heard?
Jane, what about me?
What is the word?

So Much I Looked

So much I looked at you,
my eyes filled with you
until you were all I saw.

Shape of body. Pouting lips. Long legs.
Hair shining brown in golden light;
always magnificent, especially unkempt,
when it fell over the left eye peering
at me exactly as you would have me
there . . . in the night . . . alone.

Tears

Soft as the simile of the sea from which we swam,
like the liquid tides, nothing holds them back
from where we look out upon all we look out upon,
these, Jane, the simple salt and water reminders,
unlike the aging bodies from which they flow,
never age, are always timely tokens from becoming
what we became when we leave the past behind.

Telling Jane Why I Write

I pursue the mystery of creativity
to stay inside the game without
expectation. Reality is its own
summary of meaning without
selling my soul to the devil,
explaining the inexplicable,
or subscribing to the metaphor
that reduces appreciation of the
sudden explosion of genius.
At the time and in retrospect,
I understand my vision,
its direction given freewill,
that readers desire to possess
my words, that real style is
the invention of style, that
surprising images emerge
in continuities, and that words
fill with death to remain alive.

Tryst

Filled then with lust and longing
for tingling skin and flashing eyes,
we meet and laugh away the inevitable,
lace our fingers in our locked hands,
walk into winding of our wicked words,
aware of the many dangers menacing us,
and yet we succeed where all possible
failures fall away to simplify suspicions
that we did not hear and never knew
of the causes catastrophes collect,
so casual with care we are as we fall,
each into the alarming arms of the other,
onto that bed of aspiration become ambition.

The Well-Known House

This house, Jane, I know it well.
Now this yard and those nearby are empty
of trees. The whole block has bright
sunshine where once was only shade.

Ah, this house, how illuminated it is.

On the door hangs an angel of ceramic welcome,
and the porch opens out onto the street.
Inside and on the white fireplace mantel
rests old great grandfather's revolver.
Two stained glass French doors open
upon a dining room with a wood stove.
On the English oak table there, I write
many poems about our lovemaking
in that brass bed in the room just
off this one down the nearby hallway.

All that furniture must still be somewhere.

All the brass bars of that beloved bed
now tarnish in the terrors of time.

One shady September afternoon, you leave
on the excuse of temporary city business,
a departure that makes itself permanent.

Autochthonous Jane

Jane wants me to meet her French friend.
He loves a girlfriend of hers. He might
be different with men, Jane says, but
he has a great interest in Native
Americans. I say, I could say, I know
a lot about Native Americans. Some
of my best friends are Native Americans.
But that sounds patronizing. Yes,
she agrees, You should say, Some of my
very best lovers are Native Americans.

Only later in her absence, I recall
that Jane descends from Pocahontas
through the Randolphs of Virginia.

Pocahontas is upon us:
she will forever haunt us.

More Jane

Fast Past

With this now the powerful dream allied
until fired with the experience blond,
like a poisoned man filled with arsenic,
I too left the screen door unhooked beside
a small window, shaped like a diamond,
thereby framing face while both lips I lick.

Jane did not think about arriving here,
all that silence before I could respond
(until courage to the sticking place can stick),
and I can call up words fast and clear:
Be quick!

Jane in Bronze

The beach bronzes you, Jane, beyond
the dark dusk of dependencies.
Neither speak just now nor lie
in words. Stay supine in the sand

ground from the gravel of time.
Your cock is my conundrum.
You undo me and leave me undone.
I pant like a galley slave at dawn.

When you straddle me with the waddle
of your moan, your tongue taps my teeth
and tortures me into exhausted breath.
Hold that pose and do not relax.

I will reshape it from the wax.
My monument outlives your death.

Jane Juggles

Jane gives me a black and white
photograph of herself juggling
three balls, two white and one
black. Her eyes are on the balls.
She smiles, of course.
    Jane juggles
everything: her boys, her Spanish,
her rowing, her weight lifting, her
job, her friends and sisters—Darlene,
Susan, Talbot, Amy—her husband,
her lover,
me.

Jane Lives Anne's Life Vicariously

I'm quite dull these days. I love
living Anne's life vicariously.
She just finished with one not-
made-for-her carpenter with
one child and one ex, and may
have started in on another. The
carpenter contends (frequently)
that coffee, meat, and a diet low
in vegetables are the roots of
all societal ills. His child does
not go to St. Stephen's (he's not
that bright), and this carpenter
has even less of a pot to piss in
than his predecessor. I listen to
Anne talk about how she
wants him to kiss her. She's
not particularly stimulated by
talking with him, or to him, or
listening. He is a much-
involved Cajun Dancer. And
Anne is a dancer, albeit of a
different ilk. She describes how
she shows up at Antone's tonight
with another guy friend (an
occasional dancer) and in that
way was prepared if the carpenter's
many admiring dance partners
took all his time and attention.
Anne describes this and every other
minute interaction with the carpenter
(who's still working on her porch—
are you surprised?) each of the three
times a day she talks to me for the past
five. I tell her, You are really bored by
the guy, so why let yourself get too hot
and bothered? OK. They've kissed
as of last night. Anne really gives it
the dreadful females' thorough once-
over. Translation: She's not over-

whelmed. She thinks of the first
kiss from the last boyfriend. She
compares. It too was forgettable.

The second get-together took off
(straight to hell in a hand basket,
she laments, not putting two and
two together). Direct quote (day
before the kiss): Why can't we
skip this flirtatious stuff and go
straight into involvement, so I
can start bitching at him about
how I want him to change?
Sounds like she said it in jest,
but it's sort of the truth in . . .
all this for a bit of a port
in an attention-deficit storm.

Jane on the Frontier

There's only this between her and me:
Her skin is the border of her body,
la frontera in Espanol, and yet
I'd take it on a bet if she were wet
that agua in the light shines *oro,*
rojo, and blinding *amarillo.*
The distance doesn't seem far,
but for luck I conjugate *chingar.*
My destiny here remains clear:
I cross myself and then the frontier.

Jane Plays "The Nearness of You"

Jane plays "The Nearness of You,"
but I am far away. I say, I have
tuned the piano in anticipation
of your return. She's ready.

She reads The Wind in the Willows
to her son. I talk about Mr.
Toad's Wild Ride. I speak of Toad's
mansion with all of its chimneys
in Disneyland. She says, I have
never been to Disneyland. Not
even to Disney World. Her
friend thinks all that is the
devil's work.
But Jane knows
better. Susan has the devil's
number. When you dial it,
it doesn't ring the Disney Studio.

I wear my Mickey ears. Wednesday
is Anything Can Happen Day.
Nothing does. I am far away, but
Jane plays "The Nearness of You."

Jane Reconciles Herself

Try as Jane may to reconcile herself
to the possible

(A gyroscope losing spin,
while I undress,

a sheaf of poems in hand
that I commence

reading aloud to her
randomly for the sound

of my Oklahoma accent,
and then give narrative

prattle about my art
with the locus of my life),

only the probable
interest she shows contains
the words in my heart.

Jane Refuses My Invitation to Belize

OK, sweetheart (Honey, I'm telling you
I say sweetheart to you differently than
you say it to me. But what the hell! I
think you understand . . .) What about
my Spanish? I don't want it to slip
away. I know you've talked about Belize,
but I don't think so. I've only got two
real weeks. One will be spent driving
up to see Dad (ooh, that's be a bit of
a dreary drive, but I'm determined to
save some dough). The other *con hijos*
doing something to keep my Spanish
from evaporating entirely. I'm going
to Mexico willy-nilly in the heat of
the summer. I don't even care if there's
another adult with me. We're going to
fly to Cancun, rent a car, spend a night
or two in Merida, then the rest in Akumal.
I love that beach. Or at least those are
this week's plans. We'll see (Roo dear).

Jane Sees the Difference

Considering now that there is much indifference
on my part toward you—she speaks seriously.
Indifference? What else did I expect?
She holds that body and its beauty,
she writes of my longing daily in her diary,
and she tells her friends I want only her.

Her friends love their own lovers; her interest
is not theirs. They are not able as she is
(nude in her emotions) to give a performance
to a life she could not live, could neither
conceive of nor apply herself to as much.
Are they not Americans after all?

Everything in acquisition, dear Jane.

Jane Speaks of Mexico

Ah yes, sunny Mexico.
It is. The people are
wonderfully friendly.

I think the same about the French.
I thought the same about the Italians.
I never think about the Germans.

I never mind making a complete
fool of myself trying to speak
in the other languages.

I loved lounging in the hot
well-fed series of covered pools
at La Escondido, and the road
from San Miguel to Guanajuato!

The two-hour drive was a rather twisty,
turny, guardrail-less, mountainous
two-lane climb to the most
European of all Mexican cities.

The man I was with?
He fears old age as much,
if not more than, I fear death.
He looks in the mirror many

times each day while running
his fingers through . . . his
ever-greying hair. He's not
vain, just unsure he's present.

Hasta babe,
she says as
she hurries out the door.

Jane Writes Her Dream

On the reverse of business
stationary, folded twice, and
labeled READ ME QUICKLY,
Jane writes her dream:

I meant to tell you about
the dream I had. There's
no sex in it, and the dream
has no plot. Surely,
I should stop right there.

The lighting was shadowy
with only a few slices of sun,
what you would get
if standing in the courtyard
next to your window.
I
(main theme here, how can
one help it unless dreams
forecast events?) am happy
because I had been writing
some really good stuff.

At one point (who knows
where? On the way to
a basketball game? No,
but some game may have
been the destination),
you sat beside me
in a car with open
windows; only our
shoulders touched,
and that was a relief.

You were guiding.
What you were guiding
I SWEAR I don't know.

So there. So what?
It wasn't too
inflammatory a dream.
Somewhat comforting,
however, and almost
as pleasant as
a swimming pool.

In real life
my stroke
is very fluid.
My husband
envies it.

Are you sitting
in your office
(at 1.30 this pm)
eating beans
from my (s)poon?

Or would you rather
be . . . rather be what
on this desultory afternoon?
I'd rather be off
this (small) edge
(noticed when I indulge)
of flirtation.

Am I wasting your time?
No. You'll simply
realize (if you ever
think too hard about it)
that my own behavior
(certainly possible in other
circumstances) is not
exactly an attractive trait.

Maybe you'll think,
Gee, this woman will
be much cheerier
and less edgy when
that ☐ust cloud
ascends from her
[repeat] desultory soul.

By the boxed *x* she writes
Guess what letter instead?
I'll give you 19 guesses.

I write so unabashedly.

Please forgive and
dance as much as
possible this weekend.
All switched from
1st to 2nd to 3rd person.

The 3 words a woman
wants to hear most
in the world: want to dance?

Sure.

Jane's Alarm

Jane felt no alarm when she read
the prophecy of the Ouija Board:

Let you fear the twenty-five years.
Twenty beyond, she's already passed.
She's forty-five. The term that beauty
had already allotted her far exceeded
the warning of those weary words.

So she will return to Austin slightly tired,
but wonderfully satisfied from the purpose
of her trip to Tennessee, all those days
of sensual delight in the bedroom,
the shower, the kitchen, the parlor,
and evenings spent in her lover's arms
in repeated satiation with his body.

Jane thought these thoughts. And
in Missouri, a beauty smiles in secret,
thrills herself, this young woman who
now counts her own age as twenty-five.

Jane's First Note

On a post-it,
she asks, What
do you want
the most? Peace
of mind? Spell-
checking? Or
italicizing?

I don't know
much about
word processing.

I hope you'll
come back
and talk to me.

Jane's Fortune

How unfortunate, given your beauty
its demand of how it shapes your body.
I am undone always in your presence
with neither encouragement nor success:
You are saying no, I am saying yes.

I am now your drawing left unfinished,
incomplete in the awful abstinence
you call forth in subtle indifference.
Writing it after so much has been said,
puts it down so ever it can be read.

If you on some frightful day were to yield,
I feel skin against that of mine revealed
in troubled tasks of heavy, molten lead
plummeting fast against all resistance.

Jane's Island
No [wo]man is an island.

Jane lies the length of the chaise lounge in her bikini and says,

I'm hanging out on my mostly sunny little beach.
No doubt on my mostly sunny little island.
I'm resting my eyes by locking on the horizon.
I spot a couple of ships now and again.
I imagine one might be coming my way.
Why think much about it without knowing the direction?
Sometimes I head offshore with mask and fins
(I get to look at that incredible dappled underwater light.).
I take junkets in floppy little non-seaworthy craft
with a native whose language I understand dimly.
Mostly I stay put and explore the territory,
Galapagos-like, if you ask me. I love correspondence.
I must make some sense of the bottled notes I receive.
I must know whether my island sits/fits in the scheme of things.
Hmm. Think it's a shifting plate? Maybe it's hardly an island.

I bring Jane a cold bottled water, sit on the edge of her chair,
lean forward, look down into the depth of her dark eyes and say,

I am with you there on your beach. I am your beach here.
(Where you are, even only in memory, the sun always shines.)
If I am your horizon, I rise to you and never fade.
I see the ships coming your way, but I also set
depth charges for enemy submarines you ignore.
I am one of the boats bringing with me my own portable storm.
I once again leave my West and travel toward your East.
I long to be the sea that laves your body when you dive.
Do you see reflections of me in the glass of your mask?
When you board my dangerous little dinghy, you
neither recognize me in my native disguise nor
fully translate my glossolalia except as incoherent babble.
I become the territory you explore, your Tierra del Fuego.
I correspond with love. Each day I release dozens
of bottled notes, many illisible and all addressed to you.

Placing you in situ, my function as always is to
accommodate your fit to the world. Tectonically,
the plates shift, two islands come together forming one,
where all is told and where there is no atoll at all.

Jane's Spigot

Jane brings me a spigot
and says, *Turn me on.*
Through the kitchen window,
I study the burned-down
house next door and
wonder where the neighbors
went. Jane spreads melted
butter on the black toast
she has made from the bread
she brought with her.
I pour more coffee and
offer her strawberry jam.
She accepts, but it makes
her lips sticky. I get
stuck there with the last
cigarette I light and
the tale I tell of proper
ways to peel bananas.

Jan(I)e

Janie still sleeps with her husband, but they divorced years ago. She says her friends tell her she should not do it, but she still loves him. Janie's house is like a boat beached against a hillside that overlooks a dry creek. All the windows look out to the sea. She lined the steep steps leading up to the front door with hundreds of rock specimens. She had boxes of one kind shipped all the way back here to Texas from Seattle. Janie is a geologist, but she prefers these for their shapes or colors or perhaps those also for the memories of the days she discovered them. When Janie plays the piano, the windows and doors hardly contain her joy. As the wind blows the branches of the trees—there are so many—wave silently beyond the window glass. I sleep on her couch with my feet on the armrest. When she starts up the steps to the front door, a series of connections from the foot board of the first step work their nautical way through the under structure of the house to the floorboard under the couch and the armrest moves. That is when I know Janie is home.

Memphis

When you start on your journey, Jane,
to Tennessee, know that the road lengthens
into a praise that is filled with music.
Do not fear the Nashvilleans
or Jackson and his legacy.
You will never meet him on your path,
but you will know that he has been here.
And these people are the people, yours.
Better Jackson than Crockett or Forrest.
Do not carry them within your mind.
Hope that the road you travel is long,
that the lovers you meet are many,
that you will know them for what they are
with such pleasure, with such joy!
Stop at the souvenir shops
and purchase fine mementos,
freshwater pearls, carved curios,
and fresh fruits of all kinds.
Buy as many peaches and apples
as you can. Visit hosts of southern cities.
Learn from those you seek to teach.

Always keep Memphis fixed in your mind.
The blues city is your ultimate destination.
Do not get too much in a hurry.
The best cities must be known slowly,
like the rivers they lie beside, or how
you walk their streets in your dream,
not expecting Memphis to offer you a song.

Memphis gives you the beauty of destination.
Without her, you would have stayed home.
But a city can only give you a place.

And if you find there accommodation, Memphis
serves you in providing you with herself,
what you by then will know she means.

More than a Couple of Lines

As I lie here, dear Jane, upon your breast,
my cheek feels, my ear hears your beating heart.
Last time, when? Last week? Do you remember
how you unzipped my pants, stroked my member,
found a rhythm until your hand I filled
and with your tongue you lapped with greedy lick
until our movement stopped and breathing quick
you lapsed with me until swallowing thrilled
you to iceberg ice and fiery ember,
hot as July and cold as December?
I know well you do, and as for my part
what might have been only good was the best.
So as you go ahead, I fill you full,
as in this couplet we are a couple.

Neither

It is neither in a blue china cup
I want to taste you and drink you up,
nor on palate pleasing pewter plate
that I want you to be the one I ate.

I want to bite you, lick you with my tongue,
follow the folds of your flesh where they lead,
neither return until I've met your need
nor stop singing until your song I've sung.

It is neither on yellow hardwood floor
nor upon the green of some grassy ground;
I want you in my bed behind closed door
where you love me hard until you have found

that naked there with me, flushed to red,
I have taken yours in joy of my tongue,
and your mouth smiles after giving me head
when bells are ringing though none have been rung.

Once in a Blue Nude

When I take the view
of the leg gaped you,
like this once in a blue
moon, then I know who
I want to do
when I know you
en la nue bleue.

The Only Response

Chuckle, light giggle, or belly deep
of that which reaches to the toes,
bent over with into lost control,

sometimes from smiles springs into allness,
if hard enough to the other extreme of tears,

and, Jane, for a moment everything is funny
or all madness or something so sad,
so hopeless, the only response is laughter.

Packed

Here order is ordered.
    Containers capture
the catalysts of prophecy.
All bought and
paid for, your actions adapt themselves
to time and place.
Where's the window
that wears your wristwatch?

    Jane, each
enduring yet silent, tick (its crystal clear),
final in your fear, forebodes the signature
upon the form that until your scrawl
seemed silent snow or quiet milk.

The Passing of Trains

That night I awoke again to the passing of trains,
perhaps the I-Central you rode to New Orleans,
where arriving in the morning you walked
to the square and had coffee and beignets
before searching the antique shops on Royal,
where you bought an ancient toy train,
simulacrum of such that slid these rails
the same now some hundred years ago in
that night I awoke again to the passing of trains.

Using Frank's First Lines in Attempt to Seduce Jane

From near the sea, like Whitman
my great predecessor, I call,
full of passion and giggles,
Hate is only one of many responses.
Have you forgotten what we were like then?
Shall we win at love or shall we lose?

Ah Jane Dubuffet,
Ah Nuts! It's boring reading French newspapers:
All fears, all doubts and even dreams
alone at night become profligate as if I were blonde.

An element of mischief contributes
actors with their variety of voices,
an idea of justice that may be precious,
and tomorrow morning at 8 o'clock,
as happiness takes off the tie it borrowed from me,
at last you will tire of being single.

At night Chinamen jump
avarice, the noose that lets oil.
Oh my dear oh,
be not obedient of the excellent.
Behind New York there's a face,
blue windows, blue rooftops.
*Connais-tu peut-etre la chanson
anciene "C'etait un estranger"?*

Entraining in the parlor car,
exactly at one o'clock, your arms
broach 515 Madison Avenue.
For instance you walk in and faint.

From behind I take her waist.
I pace the blue rug, Jane.
It is the end of summer;
I set out and keep hunting,
I wait, and am not without
instant coffee with slightly sour cream.

Here I am at my desk.
I am not a painter. I am a poet.
I am sober and industrious.
I am very happy to be here.
I cannot possibly think of you.
I cough a lot (sinus?), so I
move slowly sweating a lot;
my heart's aflutter; and,
my quietness has a man it—
he is transparent.

I don't know as I get what
D.H. Lawrence is driving at.
I don't know if you doubt it.
I don't remember anything of then,
down there around the magnolias,
I have a terrible age and I part,
it is 12:10 in New York and
I am wondering, Is it dirty?
It is 12:20 in New York a Friday.
It's cutting into me on its
bareback with talons lifted.

I think of you. I think a lot about
Kruschev coming on the right day.
I know so much.
I wanted to be sure to reach you;
I watched an armory combing its bronze bricks.

It's going to be the sunny side;
It's my lunch hour, so I go.
It's too wrestling at the beach sand.
July is over and there's very little trace.

Let's take a walk. You,
like a pile of gold that this breath takes,
March, the fierce! Like a wind of garters,
if I rest for a moment near The Equestrian,
if, jetting, I commit the noble fault.

I'm getting tired of not wearing underwear.
I'm having a real day of
I'm not going to cry all the time.

Bayreuth once is even more fun
than going to San Sebastian, Irun,
Hendaye, Biarritz, Bayonne . . .

Mothers of America,
not you, lean quarterlies
and swarthy periodicals,
now it is the 27th, how
do you like the music of Adolph?

Now the violets are all gone,
the apple green chasuble,
the rhinoceroses, the cymbals.
Sands, sunsets, toilets!
Sentiments nice: The Lonely Crowd
smiling through my own memories
of painful excitement, your wide eyes
so many echoes in my head.
Oh! Kangaroos, sequins, chocolate sodas.
Oh, my heart, although it sounds better.
Now when I walk around at lunchtime:
Ole sole mio, hotdiggety, nix I wather think I can.

Once at midnight in the fall, when I was a boy,
perhaps to avoid some great sadness,
Picasso made me tough and quick and the world.
Now that our hero has come back to us,
prince of calm, treasures fascinating cuts on my arm.

Quick! A last poem before I go:
Poetry is not instruments,
quips and players, seeming to
send astringency off-hours.

When I was child,
I picked up a leaf.
I ran through the snow
like a young Czarevitch.

So the rain falls,
someone else's Leica sits on the table—
that's not a cross look, it's a sign of life.
The banal machines expose themselves,

the best thing in the world,
but I better be quick about it:
The cinema is cruel.

The eager note on the door said, Call me
the eagerness of objects, the ivy trembling
in the hammock, the leaves piled thickly
on the green tree, the way to be quiet,
the opals hiding in your lids, the rain,
its tiny pressure—the razzle dazzle
maggots are summary.

The Sun woke me this morning loud,
the sun, perhaps three of them,
the root an acceptable connection to
light clarity, avocado salad in the morning,
the spent purpose of a perfectly marvelous
white chocolate jar full of petals.

There I could never be a boy.
There is the sense of neurotic coherence
to be idiomatic in a vacuum,
to humble yourself before a radio on Sunday,
totally abashed and smiling,
twin spheres full of fur and noise.

Vaguely I heard the purple roar.
Wakening at noon I smelled airplanes and hay
walls, except that they stretch through China.
Yippee! She is shooting in the harbor! He is jumping.
Yes, a long cool *vindt* is pacing over the plains, and
beside it Captain Jane, you tire of my tiresome
Mayakovsky imitations. We dust the walls,
we hardly ever see the moon anymore,
we join the animals. How funny you are
today. Welcome me, if you will.

Well, wet heat drifts through the afternoon.
What a hot day it is! For what a message!
What a picture! What you wanted I told you.
You do not always know what I am feeling.
When I am feeling depressed and anxious sullen,
why do you play such dreary music?

Val Verde and Beyond

And am I all that different? Well,
yes, I HAVE to be. I'm paying no
serious attention to anybody. Thanks,
sweetheart, for all of your Everything.
But honey . . . . Anyway, we don't
have to go there. We ain't livin' close
enough by. For a change, work has
claimed an enormous amount of my
attention these days. Maybe that's
for the best of the best in all possibles.
I've made three stunning water-level
maps. I'm greatly needed for the time
being. Oh Boy. I'm off to measure
water levels in Val Verde and Kinney.
When I get back next week, I might . . .
This is not a good time for me to
think twice about anybody, so I do
my very best not to. Once or twice.

When Jane is Jan(I)e

When I
am inside
Jane, Jane
is Jan(I)e.

Yes

I give Jane my best line.
She says, This time let's
do it as you've described,

or better yet, I'll get
the two-inch, hardbound
notebook that contains

the manual (with three-
hole punched paper for
adding and deleting

materials as necessary)
explaining Just How to
Make Jane Sublimely

Happy in Bed, and Out.

After one week of sleeping
with you I was so shy
I never said how you

could make me come.
(Not that mutual satisfaction
is everything . . ., or is it?)

Why don't you get the three-
ring manual, and I'll
meet you in the bedroom?

My expertise is interpretation
of texts. Jane answers,
Yes is what Molly Bloom

says in James Joyce's
Ulysses, and you know
why she said it.

Loving and Longing for Jane

Late Fall before the Beginning of Winter

The factory hums on the other side of town.
Beneath the pink and orange of the evening Tennessee sky,
Jane dances her full height across the lawn,

shakes her breasts and touches her nipples
with the pinch of forefinger and thumbs of each hand.
The glands hanging between my thighs throb—

"You're all I ever wanted. Nice skin
you inhabit now you are everywhere . . ."

I startle awake again. Return to
the journal—this poem where I recreate
her movements and sighs from our former recreation.

Lust applauds my performance
and leaves.
I guess I'm going to have to live with this.
Squirrels run the lengths of empty limbs
that winter retrieved from fall.

Purple blossoms of the chrysanthemums planted this year
brown and crumble after the first frost.

This never forecasts the beginning of the end
or wins again for us what we have lost.

The tincture in the creamy coffee
makes the drinking worth the cost.

Four years here and I speak like a native
with the accent of my Lawrence County grandfather,
who like Huck struck out for the Territory.

I wound back in this time to this place,
all the ruse to find you
and then to learn from losing you—

Love's lessons are hard,
hard in the hardness for you
that never leaves me slack.

The inner ear stops listening
(loses my balance before taking it back),
and in the mirror I see for the first time

the way out through the lines in my face,
how they may radiate and
cross as if to mark the spot
from which I must depart
or am now just arriving at.

Walking through the woods in Oklahoma with my dad,
I saw, memorialized in the diamond patterns
a copperhead whose coil and curves
came back, brown and gold, indelible

in bronze leaves . . . "Lookout," he shouted.
"Don't stop to identify the threat,
eliminate it in the name of possibility,
and put it away into the probable."

Then he figured the odds on it, discounted them,
until I looked up. I helped him at ninety search
for his snakeskin cane, while he hobbled through the leaves
from tree to tree unaided.

Nights I think of your black dogs,
Jasmine, who smelled like the devil,

and Smokey, blackest of all,
who wagged not his tail, but his whole ass

so delighted he was that you took him
in just before you put me out.

I think of this often in Wal-Mart
wherever I am

for unlike you, they are
the same everywhere—

"predictable mediocrity"—
but still my nerves snap,

awakening, you by my side,
until my eyes open and you are gone

from the Madrid morning of some memory
(Yourself you saved;

me you never knew)
almost as if you were not there.

Prosody butterflies move through
the perennial foliage I plant here.

I cut these movements into the right
lengths, the pieces here now I hold,

the print particular to its topography

until a shadow startles.

Left so empty in your absence,
I lingered in the lateness for you.

After the last dinner in Jackson you drove home
while you told me that you could never tell me.

Taking some several centuries in arrival here,
a bitter star shone through the tinted windshield.

I thought of it as later I held you with
my tongue in your mouth, straddling you
there on the car seat, like some horny teenager.

Yeah, you held back, and I
held on . . . only as long as I could
until there was nothing left to grasp . . .

and as I climbed off you—
my head cleared, my heart
throbbed—

my hardness softened.
Sweet baby, you could feel
the temperature drop . . .

Later, I packed my suitcase,
laid in a supply of condoms,
and left the next day for Iowa.

I look at it this way:
I'd only been buying time,
and I went broke—

Till we meet again,
Stranger.

Who have you become
since then?

Listen, I think I hear
the Belgian National Anthem

*as the wind soughs through
the icicles in the trees.*

It's much colder there.

Duplicities

I am not the same
person now I was then.
You would not know me—
What I told
you then, the truth no longer matters.
The falsehoods I fashioned
from the forge of my past
substitute themselves now for what really happened—
        I exchange one incident
for another and I protect the guilty, myself.

        With me
you must offer willingness
        to accept words
I say as I desire to speak them—
I connect no
reality to this present, but shift
        it always
to change the understanding of *that* past
        I no longer accept.

It's not that I don't have any truths,
        but I prefer secrets;
in reality, what's left's only the husk
        of the heavy grain of fact—
So I suit logic to my purpose, tell many
stories, fill them all with possibility—
suggest some probability—but not quite:
        I lie in such lies, the sum.
But for the expression on your face,
the confusion in your voice,

all delights me to smiles . . .
Sometimes when I'm exhausted
I dream those dreams I cannot describe.
For in these dreams that are not
true remains the kernel of truth
that I despise,

but then I forget
what I've remembered:
To be all women at once
without being a woman at all,
and I escape that danger; I change subjects
so my world will not do you in.

These duplicities aren't the real truth now.
All changes changed
right before I gave you my heart in gilt,
a lumpy bundle, and wrapped
in crinkled purple tissue paper—so warm to hold! My fingers had
insisted "Touch me," but when you touched,
I pulled back as if stung,
an act I repeated repeatedly.

Off balance, stumbling, ready to fall on the ready pavement,
I preferred you then discontented,
clever, yet crying and confused.
What I had marveled in our making
that I made of you, the one to hold
me close, to never let
me go, but never any closer let you hold me
for the unworthiness I posit between us.

The details now absorb me in a way I knew not:
                Like love, what I
sought, what I led you to believe,
                the year passing,
and I changed all the names,
                or spoke generally,
and when you questioned the facts, suggesting kindly,
of course, some discrepancies
in my presentation I insisted only that emotions could
be felt and never explained.

I hint we still have a future—
one for which I will assume the responsibility.
You are no longer a part of this.
Only I can be responsible.
Every night in your sleep I'll make my visitation
for I am in control.

When your semen spurts for me, I really
don't care anymore.
And every time you phone, I will neither
answer nor return your calls—
such exhilarating events, so clever and contrived!

I'm not afraid to use them in real life.
At work
I will receive my promotion to corporate
and there's talk
I'll be vice president before I'm fifty . . .
but I don't have to tell you anything.
I watch television alone in my bed, or listen
to Al Green and drink Merlot.
I wear my stubbornness like a badge,
without worrying
whether there'll be a tomorrow to work
or another day with or without you.

Not that it does matter,
but that I will make it not so,
by making it as I will—
          I am completely free.
You no longer threaten me in your goodness
or compromise my position
with your sincere and simple loving kindness.
I know nothing—
these constructs outside my being and experience—
if you sing me a song, I will laugh;
I will indulge you that I am happy,
but my father knows better than that.

And always I handle amazement with the minor efforts
of all that I've found false—
the love that I pretend to have for my mother,
my children's smiles and their even tempers.
I no longer recall the dates, but I knew you once
as one foolish enough to love me,
had I allowed it—but allowance remains my own domain.
          I will not be compromised.
In your arms, yes, I found a happiness that I had to lose.

Further Variations on My History

Why do I find it so difficult?
Don't know; it's like I'm a little girl again and
sitting at the top of the stairs and twisting my hands.

I fear going down to ask
my father if a friend can spend the night.
Why do I feel that same way when talking to you now?

Why do I not feel safe here
in your arms; just as I found no sanctuary
in my father's house, I feared also for the safety of my friend.

I don't understand why I did not grow up.
I look and feel and fuck like a woman.
Is it just that I do not know the truth?

Or rather that I prefer the propaganda more proper
to the sterility of my survival?
My clitoris vibrates out from its center to tingle my toes
 and finger tips.

I not only fucked my cousin; I married him.
And I won't speak to you of it again. I didn't in the first place.
You guessed it outright, but what did you know?
 What could you know?
Even he is not the father of all my children.

Grandmother

My dear, you will
love me, your grandmother, most of all;
alone, the stories I tell suggest our past,
the family tradition, and yes also your future.

Like you in all your dealings of the heart,
I practice some subterfuge by not telling all of it,
only suggesting what you might discover later.

There is that in me that is also
in your father, my son, and that
is also in you—that is how we love.

Tilt back your head into my lap,
let me rub your neck, so you'll feel better,
better for life—

One man you will love and him you already know;
he remains closer to your mother,
and him you will have to marry.

Steady here, once you have him—
with four children you'll think he's yours—
Your salvation, his dissatisfaction; he will betray you.

Mrs. McIntire? (All this will be of your own accord:
you withdraw your affection, and he finds himself in the arms
of those who will give him what you no longer will.)

No—You think the red cast to your brown tresses earns you
a long dress of purple pulled tight against your ample breasts
with which you will not suckle the children of your own womb.

After my death, you will live in my house,
I will visit you 16 years,
but I will walk out of your dreams before the second decade.

Remember this for you will have no photographs of me to remind
you: When drowning in the whirlpool of your life,

you will throw yourself away into the arms
of a confessed born-again Christian—careful!

You will make him love you—
and your body has the power to get you that from any man—
and then,

knowing that you cannot ever deserve his love—
you cast him into an obvious oblivion, put betrayal
in his actions because you can no longer act them out yourself.

Beware here most;
sometimes when you break a loving man's heart,
he may threaten your life. Not to worry, you will destroy him.

Always best by yourself,
nights alone in your bed,
you touch yourself and
imagine him in your arms.

Teach yourself to copy, and—for intentions utterly
beyond your dark control—how to reassemble life;
later, you become unrecognizable even to yourself.

The world promises
appearances to fashion themselves most from actions—
You will not always suit the deed to the word.

You smile and hug me close, and
perhaps you now know all there is,
"Nothing you'll ever need."

Love, too. That last morning
on your way to the hospital,
knowing you wouldn't be allowed to visit

—I was about to die, you knew that!
You came and hoped I'd tell you the rest.
... Which means you should have told me:
Life has no surprises, if you know it all.

Je regret— you are already halfway through your life.
Lust still chases after you, slowly, shouting ahead,
so that your lovely stories, lovelier lies, will all be told;
you will spin.
You think your life will never let you go.

When you find him? Damn you! your true love, you'll know.
You will love him in your way—
until he must, of course, hate you
or die.

Love's Last Lesson: Loss

> *If the Form Vanishes*
> *Its Root Is Eternal*
>   —Mario Merz in Neon, Venice

> *When night and day have had their way*
> *and all that is known has been said and done*
> *what is there left in life but love?*
>   —Georgia Temple

Lasting we thought it, yet it did not last.
Here my knowledge and the subjectivity
with which I engage you both
creates and sustains my humanity in it.
Without the possibility of constraint,
which I challenge, transgress, and
refuse, I render certain ways of
being and knowing as unthinkable:
I imagine a future horizon where
our lives can be remade from this.
Out of the susurrus of (e)motion I cast
about for the intention in your coming
here where the horse becomes the emblem
of an entourage that also invests the constructions
of man and his prismatically fragmented components
that arise from the envelope of atmospheric light.
The cultural hero claims the similar prerogative
of representation in equestrian sculpture,
where the horizontal movement of horses
against the vertical thrust of the houses provides
a momentum into the image not available
when the motor car is the means of transportation.
After you took from me the crystalline structure
of the amethyst and *las noches de amor*, you bought
out Botticelli, not just the game, but the entire
referent as symbol of artist left behind in the dust
shaken from the silver Peruvian bracelet. Such
appropriations!

                        Not satisfied to leave me, you
left me with the memory of the things you took,
so that when I sensed them again, the song, the
dance, the photograph, the bit of purple
ribbon sticking out of the desk drawer,
you knew this was a way of having me
in abstentia forever. Trapped within archetypes,
motivated by motifs, collected in the collective
unconscious, you spend your life searching
for something or someone to jolt you alive
until the velvet muscles give way to
something missing on page 87 of your biography,
and you dream that wish that the heart makes.

Petrarch was wise not to fuck or fuck with his Jane!
Se la forma scompare,
la sua radice e eternas.
Perhaps what she really said was Pet Rock.
We made our history not by the mind,
but by the heart. Here I create this place
in which to think I desire ultimate dialogue
with you who may never be my reader.

Last Love

The world's so beautiful,
and I am so sad in it . . .
Restless I was, not so tired of love
as I was of loving, because older
now, wisdom ruled my old heart
and I knew I never again would love.

All this before the special day
when I remembered meeting you a year before,
and I phoned you then—
I asked you to dinner on Saturday night,
and you said yes without any hesitation.
I arrived at seven, knocked on your
door and handed you a teddy bear.
You introduced me to many of your several children.
Later I will ask you just how many there are . . .

I open your door to my red Volkswagen, and
I admire your legs as you slide into the seat.
At the restaurant we order steaks.
You drink some house Merlot.
We watch a fashion show while I drink water
and tell you some of the tales of my alcoholism.
Over seventeen years sober in my revelation,
I know I'll tell you everything,
but I do not recall realizing at all
that you would tell me nothing,
never knew that as you stopped
at the end of each breath you breathed
you drew in the next only to further
shape it all for your fantastic fictions.

You have me already, for I'm already
imagining what it's like to kiss you,
to hold you in my arms until all is touch.
Then I am not certain where I am anymore—
Suddenly I will believe this for a long time,
for I have entered a path of a new direction,
that no retracing of my steps

can return me from, not so
much as there was no turning back, as I
knew no other way to go
as I fell forward to a place I'd never been before.

I'm not certain I'll ever know myself again,
never see Larry,
when a chance I mistake for an act of grace
puts you in my arms and you love me.

I bring myself inside you, forget my name,
as I whisper yours in your ears.
You say, "You sound like a wonderful man.
I know I'll never have to worry about you."

Once his wife, you never again speak of Michael,
he, your mother's cousin—I guess when I say,
"Why do you not want to talk about him?
Was he your cousin or something?"
So I tease you and tell you this—
That if your children tire of being siblings
than can opt for just being cousins.

But you admit your choices have genetic dangers—
once again near tears, I hold you close
and never so again mention these subjects to you.
Only later alone, I will
often chill and empty my feelings into the pit of my stomach
that you would reproduce yourself relatively.
I did not know then that this was the way of your family.

Long after I discover tears for all this,
putting you behind me, as if you could end it,
just as one finishes a kiss or a family fuck . . .
I pull back from months of your embrace—
But suddenly you seem confused:
You dismiss me in a way that begins
a pattern you will always repeat—

"I will not be here forever, you know that?
In two years I will leave here and move to Europe,
for that has always been my dream."

I think nothing of that and give you the wrong answer:
"Great, I've always wanted to live there. I'll go with you."

                    Between us never a harsh word,
and the only minor concern was yours,
that given my experience with so many lovers
you fear that you will never trust me, for you
never knew that in loving you
I would never
love another, never desire to be with anyone else again but you—

Awe and respect fill my vision:
Jane already has me
even before the waiter brings the check.
I kiss her cheek and hug her
at her front door, turn and walk away more alive than ever,
more in love than I ever thought possible in this my good life,

failing, I'm afraid to say, to see
as I'd turn my back that her
lovely face shifts into a skull,
which can only smile forever;

My awe equals Jane's anger—
for the evil of her other men, she will hold me accountable.

TO MY FATHER

> *Where shall I find comfort in my longing?*
> *There are no dreams, for there are no nights of sleep.*
>
> —Classical Chinese Poem

Father, this day
as on every other day of my life,
I love you.

Not as the small boy
who sat on your lap
those summers when you wore cool,
seersucker pants and crisp, short sleeve shirts,
and you smoked cigarette after cigarette
always alert and careful
so that you never accidentally burned me—

To satisfy your mouth
you smoked the Chesterfields and
you told the stories that taught
me to care and love
my mother, my brothers,
and you, and all this as early lessons
in love one day I
then will practice in care
for the love of a lovely brown-eyed woman;
the last time I kissed her,
my penis throbbing hard against my zipper:

"You cannot do it;
you cannot go on.

Creates
then she this sentence for you:
'Wicked women naked do fucking love to please.'
so that you might ponder its meaning,
rearranging the syntax of the words,
going that far;

and that the search in these words
brings you in the end
only the nothing she intended—

Struggle in your absence from her
and remove yourself you will from the glory of her presence.
(The purpose of all stories, you
later learn, is that
all characters, like humans, fill with yearning.)
You will know that love hurts,
but when the beloved becomes relentless in her selfishness,
she knows. She knows the truth will release you. She prefers
to hold you in pain rather than to release you with it.

You will never recover from this;
this woman who communicates for a global corporation
will never communicate the truth of her love to you.
You live with her and her husband for six months—
she has not seen him in ten years—
yet a decade later
he holds her heart with a hate she could not release,
though you think she tells you once
that she knew not sex until you
took her to your bed and loved her there,
read her the stories—sometimes thrice a week—
and continued to seduce her with
your erotic poems about
the sexy Jane of your imagination:

Suddenly one day you will stop.

Later you realize that you did all the talking;
this she encourages, your beloved, for it
frees—frees her— of speaking of
anything that matters,
and you know, my son, having had
your turn with alcohol and gambling
that in fact only the truth matters
when it comes to the matters of your heart.

Like the sour surprise of biting
into a green Granny Smith apple,
what you taste on her lips sweetens only momentarily,
and at the next taste it sours again.
The absence of the television in her childhood home
will seem curious to you; she says
the maid allowed her on occasion,
when her mother and father were away,
to watch *I Dream of Jeanie*.
The year is 1965,
but she will know nothing of the cooperative
capers of *Hal Roach's Little Rascals*.

There is a little about all that you don't know.
She will bring you books you'll love to read.
She will puzzle you often far into many nights.
She will change sleep for you."

I was born in 1951.
She was born in 1958.
You wanted me to be anything but a teacher,
a writer of stories and poems.
You desired for me monetary success—
I am certain that no one else
has ever doubted that you meant well.

Father, today, I love you. In loving my mother,
you teach me how to love Jane.

Cigarettes

I am a non-smoker . . .

—Learning
how always the last to learn,
not what to do, what not to do,
like Jane, not so much that she lied,
but more she only left the truth unsaid.

What you tell yourself:
"If you have to give her up,
you may as well give up smoking."
Victory always seems to end in surrender.
My tongue, not neutral with the taste of tobacco,
she sucked it, took in the nicotine herself,
so that before and after sex together
what we like to string out through a long afternoon
or late into a never returned from night,

you knew then you could hurt
no more than you then hurt.
That last morning you put out
the last cigarette
in the ashtray on the after breakfast table,
and as your therapist required, said aloud:

"I no longer smoke cigarettes,
and I no longer love Jane."

But suddenly one's easier
than the other . . . or you
can only utter the first part
knowing nothing will last,
neither the first
nor those that come after all is lost,
extinguished one after another,
like a tirade of falling stars,
or one cigarette after another
from a pack, one pack after another,

one carton after another carton,
a never-ending habit you do not
so much break as your heart breaks
from knowing you'll never stop
loving her, this Jane you long for.

Jane's Laughter

fills her voice as she responds to everything you say.
At first, noticed, and later, it is all you live to hear,

and your heart tells you you want to hear her forever.
You can't wait for the days to pass—

All you have the longer you have it with her, with no directive
against danger in those days; as long as it lasts you want it to last.

You desire that your heart endure duration.
For there is nothing about her you do not like:

Disagreement doesn't just disintegrate,
it does not even appear.

What you don't know then you know now,
one only steals love from sorrow,

and with a love like this,
your suffering will know no tomorrow.

You break off a little piece of happiness, your moly,
and make your descent into the underground wholly

fearless as the hero you are,
and in your truck you drive the length of Tennessee . . .

Your whole biography's locked up in her will—what
surrender you made to her without any concern for yourself!
You hope if you keep writing these words down
you will find the way to put her far behind you.

When you can't find them anymore your difference may
decide how you may disappear finally into your work.

You thought you'd seen everything, but felt
nothing for you had never felt this
impossibility impinge itself upon your identity.

But she laughed about what?
I keep asking myself—

Sexy, beautiful, intelligent,
at forty-two she looks ten or twelve years younger—

You recall when she said:
"I couldn't find a man before who'd tell me such stories,

to entertain me simply because I was cute . . .
so I made you my male Shahrazad, reversed the power,
allowed you to love me as long as your stories held out."

All indicates then merely a failure of inventiveness,
and this after all those times you took me in your mouth.

It's always the first thing you think about,
just how far down the throat you can shove it,

and how well she swallows. Her mouth, teeth,
and tongue becomes all the touch your tip desires.

And she couldn't have been pretending
about that—or when she pressed her own nipples

to her mouth and sucked herself
as hard as she had just sucked you,

so that as she wiped you from her lips
with the back of her slender hand

and said, "I know how you feel
about me. You love me. I like you,

and you know I like fucking you."
You roll her onto her back,

mount her, thrusting until she groans.
You wouldn't be strong enough for her.

When she felt about you like she never
felt before, when she got too close,

she took her fear, tore at it with her teeth
with a timeliness that filled her with terror

until she took you for one of them,
her ex-husband, her former lovers.

And if that don't beat all, trust me;
"I should have warned you about me

from that very first kiss, but please
don't blame me now for what I cannot help."

And she tells you then about the lover she had before you,
how he offered her everything and how well she refused—

She was not about to trust you for anything.
Later she will only say she cannot trust herself.

You'll see: She will write a book about passion,
a tome about loving without limits.

She directs your demise into pure data.
You won't even be acknowledged therein.

Those Seashells, for Example

That New Year's Jane returned
from the seashores of Alabama,
and I from the snowy woods
of the far northern Upper Peninsula.

While we were in our separate places,
I began to win her heart through electronic mail.
In the cozy warmth of my living room,
we sat ourselves on the loveseat—appropriate!—
and she presented me with gifts:

The page-a-day astrology calendar
(daily through which I followed our romance),
a cotton towel compressed into a palm-sized star
(Instant: I only need add water);
the thin mylar plastic fortune fish
(before my fortune became misfortune),
two books, one on the history of silk
and the other on imaginary love
(Even now you try to imagine love.),
and a hand-sized seashell that held
a handful of smaller seashells.

When she gave me those seashells,
I knew I would sleep with her.

That night in that loveseat, I kissed
her mouth, sucked her tongue, licked
her earlobes, kissed her neck and throat,
rubbing her back and buttocks continually
with my groping hands, and then slipping
a right hand inside her blouse, unsnapping
the black brassiere in the middle, and taking
her left breast, I stroked it until her nipple
hardened between my thumb and forefinger
until her fingers found my zipper and pulled
me erect from my slacks and silk underwear.

Both of us panted until we crossed the yellow
oak floor, fumbled together in pulling off of
clothes, and fell into the bed in my room across
the entrance foyer from where we had just begun.

The first fuck finds its finality
in the bright beginning of all beauty
that we create in the copulations
coming forever thereafter.

Arm in arm, we find circularity:

I remember her again this very day:
I awake alone in my bed
with my morning erection found
in the dream where I fondled her,

and I knew I never would have her again.

I hold her seashell to my ear,
and in the imaginary ocean, I hear there

again that ever hollowing emptiness
that I did not want to ever hear.

What the Living Feel

            Pain here is like pleasure,
both needed to account for and count against one another—as if
            love knew any other need except sorrow,
firm and of substance, but having the clarity of finely ground
glass; note how the light shines through the prism
casting its rainbow colors about the white wall and on the hard
wood floors with the qualities to both illuminate
and to blind those who are foolish enough in their belief to look.
            If you draw some vitality from the shame you have
allowed in the shadows of your past and in your lineage, then
you suggest the intellectual choice of how a human fails
beyond the loonier heat of the animals we have spun away from.
When I push in all my procreative force forward
with the provocative power of this semen-loaded penis, I come
for you to decide in how you will take me, if take
me into you you so desire in all the possibilities of your desires.
            Throbbing, about to burst—
beautiful in my own way
of so possessing any, some or all of the three orifices
of your body that so brings me to it,
I might just come right here where I stand. Harder to say
now just what I remember of the touch of all your body
to the touch of all my body for without one another
we are (were) nothing—
flesh without bone; or to speak further of our love,
our special loneliness apart and together;
or say I am to see you some decade from now in the crowd
of some international airport where you
rush to catch a plane perhaps to Brussels, and I am only
strolling along, taking my time, before my
flight to my long awaited holiday in the South of France.
Or perhaps home alone on some winter evening
to fill the hours, one finds that scrapbook of the year
of our love, and turning to a photograph or the words one
valued now as then in all our statements—
what might you have said
 to change it all into something other than that.
And that? That that was all that that was.

Voice

I hear her voice behind me in the hallway
calling my double name. This is the South
where such affections and such affectations
are allowed. When she says, "Larry Don,"
I know it's Jane Lynn—and I see her
standing there in the lamplight so naked.
She's on her way to the truth, dressed
for the occasion, her heart altogether
full with the spirit of loving me
in my forty-eighth year. Not completely
full, for completeness suggests closure.
She's never one to shut anything down:
"I'm not finished with you." I hear her say
it, and I am at first pleased she loves me so,
but that way leads only to a tortuous future
where the weight of this memory
will have burdened you so long in the nights
of aloneness and of never really knowing
if you can get on with the rest of your life.
Then tragedy at last strikes down
the possibility of any faith in comic relief.

Not that you deserve this. For some mornings
you will know the lilt of laughter in living,
and you will enter the crowd on a city street,
where the sun shines down warm for you.
There as the morning becomes afternoon,
you will know you have missed something,
so you try this. You write another letter
you do not mail, dial the phone and hang
up before anyone answers, or just drive
around and around the loop that encircles
this city knowing there'll always be that
within you that so needs and longs to hear her
voice that you will often conjure it up
to speak "Larry Don" or "I love you."
What you'll do next, you'll never know.

You fool yourself by making her speak
your name and other such affections
as if your imagination might prevent
her saying the name of another or saying
the same to them what she once said only to you.

Artifacts

> *For myself, who am forgotten I do not worry,*
> *But for him who vowed fidelity while he lived.*
> —Classical Chinese Poem
>
> *Belongings left behind cause delay.*
> —Chilum Railway Warning Sign

1. Prelude

From our first long embrace,
—stolen from the work of days—

collapsed I then in on myself as desire,
that dear agent of God,

allows you to undo my every doing.
I came to you becoming

and beautiful as you were and panting
in my ear as I throughout our night

returned the same to your ear,
but when we had finally done it,
all of it came down to dreaming
not the self engaged with self,
but merged yet in the mystery of the other.

Keats coughed out his love for Fanny Brawne,
and from the lamplight in the adjacent room
shadows cast themselves in the iron definition of that bed:
"I was in Purgatory with Beatrice lying there beside me."

But what the hell . . . here at 518 East Court Street,
I take you again in my arms, but you stop.

I untangle the cotton wad of the antique quilt
where you have twisted yourself,

the pattern is log cabin though we're in a frame house,
so that like some chocolate brought from Belgium

we remain so good until we melt
into one another's warm mouths.

On my way to kiss your mound
you wiggle your hips and run

your long fingers through my hair
as you push me, pull me, lower between your thighs.

2. Sports on Television

"This winter I feel the bounds of my heart
expand . . . Soon it's panties and brassieres.
I do not care if you are taller.
The distance from mouth to cock's the same."

"I want to enter you and never withdraw, never just
coitus interruptus. Always you question
my fidelity—my faithfulness goes way beyond you."

"You make me laugh by telling stories or wiggling
your naked ass as you walk from the bed
where you have been entertained by my confusion."

"I asked myself of all I'd met since I arrived
here whom did I most want to go out with?—
that's why I phoned you that ninth of December."

"I watch the Super Bowl with you at my parents'—
you hum Eric Clapton tunes while you hold
my hand so unaware of what I'm doing.
I loved you, but never like a husband."

3. Madrid Madness

She was a tall beautiful woman,
just my type, with perfect vision,
and she saw me exactly
the way she intended to see me.

—July. Madrid. Crowds. Streets
like heat to the melding of the souls.
Her hand's in mine as we crossed
the avenue where I pay our admission
to the botanical garden adjacent
to the famous Prado Museum.
Bed after bed of beautiful flowers
between the grid of sidewalks
we walk, and inside the exhibition
hall, photographs of suffering Mexico.
Back outside we follow the iron signs
that led us to potable water—
My friend, my love, there with no
memory of your husband, we take
each our slow and refreshing turn.
Drink   slowly
inhabit   this   vacancy
all   the   heart to fill.
What do I? What do you
feel?

All around us, the flowers, the foliage,
no books, no desks, no folders, no papers,
and the poem then being lived without
need of the journey from tongue to pen
to journal before the necessary word processing.

At the newsstand just across the street,
the front page colors show the running
of the bulls in Barcelona. We are here
in the capitol city, safe for now, but never
safe from what we can do to one another.

Tightly I squint my eyes
shut when the sun blinds,
and I do not hear you saying
under your breath—
You imagine I'm real You suppose   I love you
I have a gun right here in my purse   Listen, hear
the trigger cocking
My love for you just blows you away
Gypsies approach us—
their extended hands show the slickness of receiving
so many coins, more than we could ever give.
You shout, "Santiago . . . y a ellos!"

4. Conversational Exceptions

"Thank you for your love
and concern for me; it means
more than you can ever know."

"We will need to stop this soon.
I will say more to you in this poem
than I said to you in my life. I wrap
myself in the weariness of abundance."

"All had been dry so long
until I pulled on my mackintosh
and went out into the wet world,
where I drank you up in my thirst."

"Like all heroines I changed,
changed as often as I changed
clothes—the purple pull over
for the T-shirt that proclaimed
to all of Austin you were a poet."

"Did you destroy all my E-mails?
Or did you print each one, arrange them
chronologically in the portable purple file
box that you stored in your empty attic?"

5. Refusal of the Proposal

The heart beating. Ready for anything. Yes. Ideal
love does not have to be a remote possibility.
As my new found passion permits,
I take her as often as she allows.

"I love to dive," she says; and
I listen, attentive, but am never told
which reef, what ocean, the circumstances,
or the depth to which I must descend
without knowing these simple answers.
How dangerous it is to enter a narrative
in which no one tells you the truth!

"I've only loved you for a short time, for
crying out loud. I don't do this to amuse."

You still listen and when you hear her break
the stillness you do not know that she is lying
right there in your arms where you hold her—

*She delights that her twins are boys; her other children
daughters; she got pregnant so easily, she says,
but after the abortion she got her tubes tied; then
she pulls up her blouse, shows you the thin scar you
can hardly notice just above her pierced navel—*

More kisses; more cups of tea; more trips to the land
of no telephones, and as you wait for her call, you
dream a night of emptiness that comes months later . . .
Drama dying into the drama, like so many encounters
sexual in the season:

You cannot remember one from the next.

Then later that day, she leaves the message
that she cannot spend the night with you—
She drops by: "I love you so much I do not
want to leave you, so leave you now I must."

Gone. I find myself crying—
By myself? Alone? Worse. In a crowd!

Jane. Give me a break, I plead,
but she gives me a broken heart.

All's so *Seinfeld*. Sin-filled? Last year
there was a whole episode:
"It's not you; it's me."

Now it comes to us. What she brought to us.

I did not bring it.
I did not accept it.

6. Arbitrary Alabama

—May. Gulfshores. Sand. Sun.
Sea. A few purposeful porpoises
circle us as we swim the salty sea.
Your breasts bulge from your new
bikini, and I lounge later on the beach,
one eye always open, as I admire again
the beauty of your body. I grow hard
knowing I will know it each and every night,
intimately. Our sex together shows a quality
and depth of performance and achievement
rather than mere length of time
spent in a condo at the beach.

. . . A crowd in a wreck of building,
the bar straddles the state line, takes
the elision of its name from both states.
Jane, restless, holds me close,
and we dance into the depths of the drunken
crowd where all I want
is she who's close in my arms.

Having lost nature, we invent culture . . .
EACH EVENT! The surface of each
we slide in time and in space
inside each other for perfect fits,
like a matrushka stacks each doll
inside the moment of its memory.
Will it all come back to me?
I capture in these few images
then present, now lost, in which
my soul first opened . . .

She's more beautiful than you remember   Pulling her
out of your memory you guide her into the myth
music has made   in fashion   What lengths you went
to in loving her   then in the bright sun
you could see   and in the dark sun you could not see

You drive together south on 51
to Millington . . . At the art show
you introduce her to your friends;
proud of the kindness she gives
you in her praise of your paintings,
you cannot wait to show her how much.
Before noon you have her alone
in the nearby El Reyes Restaurant—
"Have you ever dived off the Turks and Caicos Islands?"
. . . Her answer; my . . . memory,
hardly now so firm, so that I shake my head.
Should I have shaken my fist?
Such is the power of pleasure . . .
How it hooks the soul
into the pain of the body!

Later, out for an evening piano recital,
I hold her hand while we sit on folding
chairs—the musician, only eleven, is
a prodigy—and afterward we take up
the same rhythm of the last piece
he played as we make a piece ourselves
from each other: The next week
while I'm in England, I desire
the bed of no woman I meet there—
I only depart from each smiling—
"But who is the best lay?"

In Deddington or Stow-in-the-Wold,
I tease the woman with me about sex with her;
I know she wants me, but I
want only Jane, long only to return
home as soon as possible and have only her,

WHICH IS EXACTLY WHAT I DO
THE VERY NIGHT I RETURN TO THE STATES

Another night . . . inhaling her perfume,
pleasures, in the king size bed at the Excelsior . . .
"We'll always have that weekend in Little Rock."
That night you tell her your fantasy:

Yourself in bed with two beautiful women,
who both look just like her, of course.
Black women whom you loved, you dream of them
that night, but the erection with which you awake
she blows you to remove:
Oh, you are so satisfied
as you tour the Old State House
and review the renderings
of the Thorncrown Chapel.

I invited her to meet me at lunch
at my house on Bissextile Day—
there we fucked and gave ourselves
the glow and glory of that nooner,
possible only every four years, and
inserted a memory into our lives
to recall some four years whence
my erection will thereafter become
an icon of an earlier time together.

It was late, then and the moon
shone through the window . . . in the living room
I pulled off her skirt and dress
. . . she wore no panties. I unhooked her bra

as I lowered her onto the Chinese carpet
where I thrust into her until she came screaming
hopeful obscenities high up the fourteen-foot walls.
Then I continued until her
breathing evened out again,
so that before I could ejaculate
into the full heat of her vagina
she pulled me out and into her
mouth where I came to her joy
and with a content that never left her.
As she swallowed . . "Hey, I love
the taste of you . . . and I don't want
to ever stop . . . Yeah, you know I'm
talking to you . . . Look, you're hard again
in my hand, so please follow me
to the bathroom. I have to go."

You follow her to the bathroom,
watch her pee as you finish a story—

In this one you are in love with a French
woman who prefers that you know her
every orifice each time she takes you down.

After she finishes and before she rises,
she reaches out and takes my penis—

pulls me closer to her and
takes me again in her mouth—

I did not know I'd come again—

June. Dyersburg. Birds sing above
the hum of the window unit
air conditioner . . .

7. Up and Down: The Yo-Yo of (E)Motion

"Our sex life could not contain
our passion; all became that,
so that abandon had to be abandoned—

And to think we'd only known each other for 6 months.

It's not just the music—listen.
When I am in bed with you—
A whole symphony plays up the crescendo of my feelings,

but you don't want everything reduced to pure emotion . . .

Love never gets any easier than sex—
Passion untamed becomes addiction."

"Sunday should always be the first day for sex the first time . . ."

It was for us appropriate as an act of grace—
the undeserved gift.

I love your tongue—what you speak with it
and how you use
it to trace the terrain of my body—

No accent accounts for the loophole in your voice,
where I fit my ears to accommodate my soul . . .

Phone me at work—I hate to think this
ends in the confusion of telephone talk."

"Today I lunch with the bank teller,
tall, blonde, and only twenty-nine last week.
I will tell her that sex with her
brings me back to her. I'll see . . .

I never think about it with you now.

What you made of my suggestion that we continue
to have the occasional sexual encounter with others
situated for me just what part your heart had
in bringing it all to this, its inevitable conclusion—

No so much that you fucked me,
but that you fucked me over."

"Talking. I was always talking to you.
I thought my doing so made us what
we were and held us together in time
before it all went crazy.

I know that if I told you
I had to stop seeing you—
even your firmly allotted 1 hour per week—
that it would be over, that it would end."

Talking. You claimed that you knew
you weren't finished with me. *It was
a way you could keep hurting me*. Stop.

8. Orality and Orgasm

I tried leaving town;
I kept coming back,
and I never saw you again,

except once pulling out
from the driveway at your father's
house, which I must

drive by both to and from
each day, going and
returning from work—

just a honk
and a quick wave
and I was gone.

The twist and roll of my days
demand constant prayer,
and when I'm not praying

for myself, I am praying for you.
I put all my belief into miracles,
but I no longer believe

that miracles will come
for me or from your dark
days of deeds and deception.

Just as late last night, 2. a.m.,
I wake to the immediate knowledge
you longer love me

enough to do the least thing
to make it work,
and compare this,

as compare I must,
with my undying willingness
to try anything, anything at all,
to keep you.

9. Traffic

> *After sex . . . we held each other*
> *close and prayed for deliverance.*

A Santana song in the pickup
I sang while waiting at the red
light at the corner of Sampson
and St. John—

I redecorate the studio,
paint it a candy red,
refinish the reddish-white pine floors,
so that I will have another room
to contain the calamity of my sorrows—

My blue leather recliner holds me—

Most evenings I watch the old movies again,
those where the lovers work against varieties of difficulties
to have their love for their love
is all they have, the lovers,
and when I dress in the morning
I select the tie to match the socks,
then socks to match the silk underwear;
when I drink my coffee with cream,
I wonder without wanting if across town
she drinks her morning cup of tea, and
if she does, when she does,
does she ever think of me.

I recall how my visits a las Convent des Huelgas
e Monasterio des Flores prepared me
for these many months of abstention.
La vida en vivo!

You know wherever you sleep tonight,
and with whomever you sleep there
that this one now so far from you
still loves with a love undiminished,
one that can neither be forgotten nor forgiven,
and the emptiness of this bed, vacant
like the hollow heart that you left him,

folds in on him with a force that
forgetfulness, try as he might to recover it,
cannot take from him the hurt he embraces.
Know that you are responsible
though he owns his part in it
and with the whole world he
shares his tears, not just for
a night or two, but always
for the rest of his many years.

"One night she was in her bed
when an old lover broke into
her house, and he forced her.
When he was finished, she thought,
he left, but he only went down
to the car to get his father.
He sent him back to screw her, too.
He'd heard about her love for fathers."

If Karl Marx had had more of a Freudian
bent, he might have said, "Even the fuckers
need to be fucked." I'd rather mention
now the Fibonacci sequence, so that all may
know that everything, even this, has its pattern.
You don't have to have the DV4DR to take
the risk for further fantastic procreations.

I value how I measure the cast of my vision,
whose role remains the determination of my destination—
"Do you believe I write these words to return to you?
I keep wanting to scream a last long goodbye,
because this is about leaving, not about loving you."

Later while pumping gasoline at the Dodger,
down there on South Main, reassurance
manifests itself in the new motto I keep repeating:

Such faith remains the substance of things—
What I hoped for, the evidence of that
not seen—no artifacts attest to its actuality.
. . . One August day
You came back to my house

to break if off, to say goodbye
for good, not
knowing I'd ask you to marry me,
not knowing you'd take a week
to say no. Nada. Nothing will
come of that nothing now.

On the floor I placed my feet firmly,
and I never asked anyone who ever turned me down—
If you don't ever finish
you don't have to do it over . . .

What was I doing there?

I select some future Monday
then to speak with you on
the phone for the last time.

"Do you think I should stop smoking?

Go away . . . please come back . . .
Please let me leave . . . Please stay."

To get anywhere together we must
first agree on the same destination,
but you want to take separate cars.

If you'd get an ocean between us
that would not be enough distance
to blend or blur the beauty of my glance
as it bounces off your breasts.

I pick up the phone often,
dial, then hang up.

A Steely Dan song in the pickup
I sing while waiting at the red
light where Lake Road
crosses Highway 51 By-Pass,

perhaps just another route around you.

10. Secrets: Confessions

> *The perpetual now is as*
> *beautiful as it needs to be.*
> —Susan Bright

You could not see it, and not
saying it kept it from knowledge . . .

   And God knows,
it was nothing you could see with the naked eye,
some dire discretion depended upon it,
to operate in a hidden manner, confidential,
secluded, and not frequented by experts—
who'd only try to make something of it anyway.
Only the initiated share such secrets.

You had already been initiated.

No disclosure beyond ordinary understanding
presented itself in the way you listened.

Something suggested confession,
called for a collapse of the code,
an avowal of faith
in a need particular only to you, the practitioner;

Like the attitude inherent in a secret aesthetics

of taking my body,
of taking my heart,
before casting away
my then-wearied soul.
Nothing clears.
No statement acknowledging guilt
spoke
you then of that your dirty little secret.

—But with everything to lose
to me, the threat to it all,
you proved it paradoxical,
something of an open secret—

"We can't—we would be too happy.
Like the abused puppy, I will never
let anyone, you included, pet me."

I know.
"You think I made this all up, like I did my love for you."

11. An Email

Dear L—

I realize now I should have shown the source of my secret
agenda, but the subversion of pretenses into the felicity of
falsehoods,
the charge of my own covert operation,
that you can no longer either cry or cry conspiracy—
I assure you that I alone was the only principal in this case.
There's something else I've been meaning to
tell you,
just as there is a meaning that is something beyond my telling,
yet needs my attention.
Getting at a hidden truth might have served
our love well;
I just did not want to allow that to happen.
Later in the hideout of my heart,
I may confess some of this to myself, but as for you,
my love, you will never know what reasons
I relinquish from the responsibility for my story.

        Love,

12. Nonfiction
> *What you've just said, if you've said it, is the truth.*

The fiction behind the fiction

   in the photograph within the photograph,
I hold a black and white photograph;
the rest is color, except for that within
that within, and like the firm folds
of lovely labia, like the labors of my helpless heart
it does all fit.
Years from now it becomes a classification
for you—the notice of a not-so-nice
reconnaissance of a past you might have
shared with me as your lover had I loved you after that,
as one on some sad summer night on
                some sandy beach near San Diego.
—Alone you will the emptiness of yearning for the simplicity of the
sea from which you may never hope to swim from . . .

The fiction behind the fiction

In "Celebration of the Last Poem,"
you will no longer need the witnesses
nor take their testaments for a truth
other than how they would have it
(I swallow now all memories of you, and
the taste leaves my lips like your last kiss)—

Once you set aside your heart
to magnify the need you had for yourself,

the touch of another's touch to yours—
what we once had between us—
nothing else matters to either of us.

You become the one without the smile
you only smiled for your father
and me; without my always distracting erection,
I might have made from this more than now,
this glance over the shoulder, the lingering then
of some past victory or how

an unanswered phone if left to ring
will finally of its own accord stop.
Now I'm in the arms of another,
or you are in the arms of your new love.

And turning: Eyes tearing in desire,
I grimace the mouth into a smile
to search for a new found sense
of humor, just for a few laughs
here at the end.

At the new beginning where the edges of this past fade,

I look neither back nor forward,
but cast my tear-bleary eyes up to the heavens
with the scrutiny of one searching
for yet another cupid—

Another fiction   then the truth.

The Extra Poem

You
I know
as

she who fucks
on the carpet
until her buttocks
burn with redness.

Years pass
like time does,
so that down
in another night
with another lover,
you will remember
me as I remember you:

Do this in remembrance of me, as
I do this in remembrance of you.

Know the aftershave I wear
as you know the perfume you
splash behind your ears, and
inhale the smells sex makes
from the helpful holes of the body;
fit all this into the largesse of your heart.
Recall the kindred sexual touch you long for.

Keep both eyes open, and always be on the look out for me.
Admire as always how age will actuate the beauty of the body.
Grow ever hard in your knowing, your learning, and your
yearning.
Listen for a voice to call out, "It's me. Find me now.
           Fuck me forever."
Alone you have already discovered the delight of loneliness,
so I leave this message should you come along behind me:

The more cups of water I drink:
The thirstier I become for your wet lips.

An Oklahoman, Griffin has one book of short stories, nine books of poetry and more than four hundred poems, hundreds of essays, and three dozen short stories in journals to his credit. His art appears in private collections in Africa, Australia, Asia, Europe, North America, and South America. For the past four years he has lived in Ras Al Khaimah, United Arab Emirates, where he serves as Professor of Languages and Literature and English Program Director at the American University of Ras Al Khaimah. In the Fall of 2016, he joins the faculty at the American Institute of Malta.

www.ingramcontent.com/pod-product-compliance
Lightning Source LLC
Chambersburg PA
CBHW070156100426
42743CB00013B/2936